Helping Children See Jesus

ISBN: 978-1-64104-106-5

God Provides
The Life of George Mueller

Adapted from George Mueller by Faith Coxe Baily © 1958,
Moody Bible Institute, Chicago, IL

Adaptation: Thomas Luttmann and Hannah Landis
Illustrator / Computer Graphic Artist: Del Thompson
Page Layout: Patricia Pope

© 2020 Bible Visuals International
PO Box 153, Akron, PA 17501-0153
Phone: (717) 859-1131
www.biblevisuals.org

All rights reserved. No part of this publication may be reproduced, stored in a retrieval system or transmitted in any form by any means, electronic, mechanical, photocopy, recording or otherwise, without the prior permission of the publisher, except as provided by USA copyright law.

RELATED ITEMS

To access related items (such as activities, memory verse posters and translated texts) please visit our web store at shop.biblevisuals.org and enter 5140 in the search box on the page.

FREE TEXT DOWNLOAD

To access a FREE printable copy of the teaching text (PDF format) in English or other available languages, enter S5140DL in the search box. Add the item to your cart, and use coupon code XTACSV17 at checkout. Once your order is processed you will receive an email with a link to the free download.

STUDENT ACTIVITES

These are included with the FREE printable copy of the English teaching text for this story. See the directions under Free Text Download (above) to access them.

But my God shall supply all your need according to His riches in glory by Christ Jesus.

Philippians 4:19

Chapter 1
DEPRAVITY AND SALVATION

George heard the slam of the carriage door outside. It was his father. He stomped inside the front door and spied George on the stairs.

Show Illustration #1

"So, you aren't even ashamed enough to hide! I would think you'd have learned some manners after spending a month in prison."

George glared back at his father. "I learned that meals in German jails are terrible, and I learned how much you care about me. You could have paid my fine a lot quicker."

It wasn't George's first encounter with the law. This time he had tried to leave a village inn without paying his bill.

His father's anger turned to grief for a moment. "You're only 18 and already a common thief, George. If your mother were still alive . . . I'm glad she doesn't have to see what you've become."

"And what about you, father?" George shot back. "You're nothing but a tax collector living off the government's money."

It was too much for his father. In a flash he grabbed a cane hanging on the wall.

"I'll teach you some respect!"

The cane cut sharply through the air.

Any feelings of guilt George might have had were quickly forgotten as he returned to his old habits. He had given in to his father's wishes for him to become a minister for the German state and was now studying at the university in Halle, Germany. However, most evenings he could be found avoiding his studies and relaxing in the village tavern surrounded by friends.

One such evening he was seated at a table telling a story when he noticed a stranger at the end–a stranger who looked familiar.

One of his companions spoke up. "Beta! Come up here and meet George Mueller! He'll teach you how to really drink!"

"I know George Mueller already," the stranger replied with a smile.

George's mind raced. Where had he met him before? It was from school somewhere. Then he remembered.

Here was Beta, the boy who never sinned. He always had his Bible and hymnbook with him, never cheated on exams and never ever drank.

Now he was seated with a mug at the table listening to George.

"Continue with your story, George," Beta said eagerly.

Show Illustration #2

Later that evening, Beta caught up with George underneath a streetlamp.

"George, I bet you thought you'd never see me here."

"I guess a little," George replied.

George was more than a little surprised. As a schoolboy, Beta had never missed an opportunity to tell George he was bad.

Beta continued, "I'm different now, George. I want to have some 'fun' like you."

George laughed. "Beta, if you only knew. I always wished I was a little more of a 'saint' like you."

In fact, George was sick and tired of all the silliness, but he didn't know how to get away from it.

"I guess we will let fate decide," he said at last. "Will you go my way or will I go yours?"

Show Illustration #3

Beta and George soon became good friends, but they both seemed to be going George's way.

NOTE TO THE TEACHER
Gospel Points

 God's unconditional love

 Jesus has risen again!

 Jesus is the only Perfect Son of God

 Will you repent and accept Jesus as Saviour?

 All have sinned.

 Application for the believer

 Jesus' sacrificial death on the cross

Throughout the text of the *George Mueller* story, we have included Gospel Point icons. Whenever you see an icon, please refer to the *Note to the Teacher* section of that page. You will find suggestions to help you explain that gospel point to your class. These points are optional with the understanding that you plan on presenting the gospel during your Bible lesson time instead.

However if this story is the only lesson being presented, please take advantage of this feature. Sow the gospel seed!

* * * * * * * * * * * * * * * * * *

It certainly didn't seem as if George and his father had a very loving relationship, did it? Do you know that there is someone who loves you very much? God loves you and He wants you to know Him.

Do you think that it was true that Beta "never sinned"? (Allow responses.) No, he may have behaved better than George, but the truth is that he was a sinner just like George. In fact that's true of all of us. The Bible teaches that you and I are sinners. In Romans 3:23 it says, "For all have sinned, and come short of the glory of God." That word all includes you and me. We have all broken God's law through our words, thoughts and actions.

– 42 –

Over the summer, along with three other friends, they hiked to Switzerland. Each had a passport signed by his parents–or so it seemed. George had carefully forged his father's signature!

Although each had money for the trip, they placed their leather pouches together in one large pouch. George was the natural choice to hold this pouch as he was the best with money and math.

Little did the others know that he was also the best at looking out for himself. While the others snoozed on grassy hillsides, George would carefully transfer some coins from each of his friends' pouches into his.

One time Beta caught George in the act.

"What are you doing, George?"

"Nothing." George froze for a moment but quickly regained his composure. "Just . . . organizing a bit."

"You're a good fellow, George," Beta said with a yawn. "Always keeping track of things. Someday your talent for money may come in handy."

Beta rolled back over to sleep.

George smiled.

After the Switzerland trip things continued unchanged until one night outside the tavern George and Beta stood again below the lamplight.

Show Illustration #2

"See you tomorrow, Beta?" George asked.

Beta hesitated.

"What's wrong?" George continued.

"I . . . I promised a friend named Wagner I would meet him tomorrow."

"Fine, bring him along. We'll have a good time together."

Beta's eyes began to bulge as if they were going to burst.

"Look here, George, when I told you I wanted to have 'fun' I didn't mean I wanted to turn my back on everything forever."

"Go on, Beta," George said.

"Wagner's having a . . . a prayer meeting."

"A prayer meeting?! Sounds like an interesting fellow," George jested.

George felt like humiliating Beta, but something made him say, "I'd like to meet him. Tomorrow in fact! Maybe I'll learn something from your goodness after all, Beta."

Wagner's house was tucked into a long row of gray stone houses within the village. George noted that it had a friendly look. At the door he was greeted with a handshake from Wagner.

"We welcome you as a brother, Herr Mueller. Find a seat and a hymnbook. We're about to begin."

Several men sat in a circle. Unlike most religious men he had met, these men seemed rather ordinary and humble.

Wagner introduced him to the others and then asked one man to pray.

What happened next shocked George.

Show Illustration #4

The man stood up and turned his back to the circle. Facing his chair, he knelt down on the hard wooden floor. George had never seen a man pray like this, not even in the state church.

The man began to pray, but again, not as George was used to hearing. He spoke to God as if He were right in that room and so close that this man had to kneel in humility, like one would before a king. This man feared God and adored Him.

George began to think about himself. What did he know of God? He had studied the Bible and could probably speak more eloquently about it than most of the men in that room, but did He know God?

His life certainly didn't show it. George Mueller said whatever he wanted to say. He thought whatever he wanted to think and did whatever he wanted to do. George Mueller was the king of his own life.

Suddenly he began to feel sick. Nothing in his life had brought the joy and peace that he saw in this man as he spoke to God.

Later that evening, George quietly made his way back to his room. Its bare walls reminded him of the emptiness in his own heart. He had gone to the prayer meeting that night expecting to sing a few hymns and to find some material to make a fool of Beta. Instead something had happened to him.

For years he had understood perfectly that Jesus Christ had died on the cross to save sinners, but this truth had never lived in his heart. Now he understood. Jesus Christ had died for him–for self-serving George Mueller! And He had done it so George could know God in the same way as the man at the prayer meeting.

NOTE TO THE TEACHER

George didn't have much respect for his father, did he? He's a lot different from another son I know. Jesus is the only perfect Son of God. He came to this earth and lived a sinless life, always respecting His Father and showing obedience to Him.

George planned on making fun of Beta, didn't he? Maybe you've had someone make fun of you because you are a Christian. Perhaps they said something that made you feel bad, or they acted differently toward you. Do you know that God cares and He wants to help you? While the Apostle Paul was in prison for preaching the truth, he wrote in a letter: "I can do all things through Christ which strengtheneth me" (Philippians. 4:13). That's the same strength God will give you as you trust in Him. If you know Jesus as Saviour, you can trust God to help you stand for what is right.

I want you to know that Jesus, God's Son, died for you too. He lived a sinless life here on earth. Unlike you and me, He didn't deserve to die for His sin because He had none. But instead He gave His life as a perfect sacrifice for our sins by dying on the cross. Jesus Christ didn't stay dead though. Three days later Jesus rose from the dead and lives even now. By trusting in Him as your Saviour from sin, you can begin a new life with the promise of eternal life in Heaven and the power to live a life now that's radically different!

Show Illustration #5

Beside his bed, George dropped to his knees. With his hands spread over his bed he prayed. His prayer was not a rehearsed one like he was used to, but one asking forgiveness of an almighty God. With a sigh, George finished, "At last! God, tonight I am Yours!"

In the following weeks, the direction of George's whole life changed. Rather than becoming a minister for the German state, George decided to become a missionary. It wasn't a decision easily made. George wondered what his father would think.

In the spring, George met a man named Hermann Ball. Ball was a missionary to the Jews in Poland. His clothes were cheap, yet George could tell by the way he acted that Ball was from a wealthy family. Eventually Ball told what had happened. His father was a wealthy merchant from east Germany. However, when he found out his son had decided to give up a career to serve Christ, Ball had been kicked out of the family. Would the same thing happen to George?

Show Illustration #6

The carriage rocked mercilessly all along the way from Halle to George's father's home. In his mind, George could hear his father's voice and the debates he knew would come.

The meeting was very important. George was applying to a German missionary training institute, but the application would not be valid without his father's signature.

That evening at dinner George barely touched his stew. There was only one thing on his mind. Finally he had the courage to place the blank application before his father.

Show Illustration #7

His father's answer was almost immediate.

"When I say 'no' I mean 'no.'"

"But why don't you want me to be a missionary?" George pleaded. "You always wanted me to be a minister."

Now his father was on his feet.

"A minister, yes! But one who earns a nice wage from the state! One who can fill the table with food at Christmas! One who can take care of a father in his old age."

George bit his lip. His father wasn't sick and he wasn't old. He had money in the bank. He was well-to-do.

"Father, may God forgive you for what you do to me today. May He forgive you for making me choose."

"And what do you choose?" His father asked, returning to his chair.

"I've made a promise to God, Father. Somewhere there's a mission field that needs me."

"But what about the application? I won't sign it!" There was almost a smile on his father's lips.

 "I will manage somehow. I'll finish my studies at the university without your help. I won't take money from you again, Father. Not as long as I live."

Show Illustration #6

On the way back to Halle, George realized he was finally independent of his father. He was on his own and free as a bird to do what God wanted him to do!

As the carriage door slammed behind him, he became aware of something else. He hardly had any money at all and certainly not enough to pay his school bill.

 From now on his dependence would have to be on God alone. Would God provide?

NOTE TO THE TEACHER

 It wasn't easy for George to talk to his Father, was it? Yet George knew that God wanted him to be a missionary, even if it meant being rejected by his father. George trusted God to do the right thing, and so can you if you know Jesus as your Saviour. Remember God's Word, "I can do all things through Christ which strengtheneth me." (See Philippians 4:13.) You can trust God to help you stand for what is right.

 How do you think God might provide for George's needs? (Allow responses.) Do you know that God has provided for your greatest need already? Through Jesus Christ, the perfect Son of God, we can be saved from the punishment and power of our sin. Maybe today you realize that you are a sinner. You've broken God's law, but you also realize that Jesus can save you because He has died on the cross to take the punishment for your sin. Not only that, but He has risen from the dead and lives today. You can place your faith in Jesus today. I'd like to give you the opportunity to talk to someone about that right now. (Give instructions.)

 Maybe you're here today and you know that Jesus is your Saviour. You've placed your trust in Him completely to save you from your sin. That's wonderful! Do you know you can also trust Him to help you to stand for what is right? He promises to give you strength.

REVIEW QUESTIONS

1. Why was George's father so angry with him? *(He kept getting into trouble for stealing and was sent to jail.)*
2. What did George's father want him to learn to be? *(A minister)*
3. Who did George meet one day in a tavern while he was away at college? *(His old schoolmate, Beta)*
4. What wrong thing did George keep doing while he was on a trip to Switzerland with his friends? *(Stealing some of their money)*
5. When they got back from their trip, where did George decide to go with Beta? *(To a prayer meeting)*
6. What did George think was so different about the way the man at the meeting prayed? *(The man knelt to pray and talked to God as if he knew Him.)*
7. In his bedroom, when George understood that Jesus had died for him, what did he decide to do? *(Ask God to forgive him and be his Saviour)*
8. After George came to know Jesus, what did he want to do instead of becoming a minister? *(Be a missionary)*
9. What did George's father say when George told him he wanted to learn to be a missionary? *(He said no; he would not sign the paper so George could go to a missionary school.)*
10. George told his father he would never take this thing from him again. What was it? *(Money)*

Chapter 2
PERSONAL DEPENDENCE AND PROVISION

George Mueller could no longer count on any money from his father. At first the thought of asking God alone for food and money seemed insane; yet the thought remained.

One morning at breakfast by himself in his room, George once again fell to his knees.

"God," he said aloud, "You know exactly what I've done and what this means. You know what I need: money for rent, for food, for books and for my school bill. I'm depending on You, God. In Your own time. In Your own way. I'll wait."

A little later there was a knock at the door. George froze for a second. A bill collector? George cautiously opened the door.

It was Dr. Tholuck from the university along with a stranger.

"Hello, George. Let me introduce Dr. Hodge from America. He's looking for a bright student who knows English and can tutor in German."

"I'd like to," George began, "but this semester I'm rather busy. I need to work . . ."

Dr. Tholuck interrupted, "But George, tutoring is work."

"I'm willing to pay the standard rate for eight hours a week," said Dr. Hodge. "The others will pay the same."

"Others?"

Dr. Tholuck smiled. "That's right, George. Three of Dr. Hodge's friends need tutoring as well."

"We'll pay separately and study together," Dr. Hodge added.

Show Illustration #8a

George couldn't believe it. God had done it. He had brought just what George needed, right to his own door. The money would be enough to pay for his school bill completely. But that wasn't all. For part of the year, George was allowed to have a free room at the Halle orphanage nearby.

George soon learned about how the orphanage had been founded a hundred years before by a university professor named August Francke. He had no money or wealthy family to rely on. He had simply prayed in faith to God. God had provided the money, and the orphanage had been built. It became a daily reminder to George of God's provision.

After finishing his studies, George spent the next several years working as a German tutor for more American students. He also continued to pray about where God wanted him to be a missionary. At first he thought God was leading him to Eastern Europe, but war broke out there and the door was closed. Then, through Dr. Tholuck, George heard about a missionary society in London. George quickly filled out an application . . . and waited and waited . . . A response came back. The society wanted more information. George quickly wrote a response . . . and continued to wait. Finally a letter arrived–George was accepted! But on one condition: he would have to study six more months in London.

Show Illustration #8b

Despite some delays, George finally boarded a ship to cross the English channel. As the English coastline came into view, George's mind filled with thoughts. How would he manage here in a foreign country? He knew a little English, but certainly not enough to carry on a conversation, let alone share the gospel. Still he was excited, especially when the city of London came into view through a maze of sailing ships. It would be fun to explore! (Show map if desired.)

Show Illustration #9

George soon found out that the only exploring he would be doing would be on the pages of books. The mission society quickly put George to work studying ancient languages 12 hours a day. For a moment George's old rebellious spirit returned, but he determined to serve those six months as best he could. Day and night he studied. The more he studied, the more cluttered his mind grew. Soon his head ached, his back ached, his neck ached. He finally realized that he was more than just tired; he was sick.

A doctor examined George and recommended some remedies, but the condition persisted.

"What you need is to get this sooty London air out of your lungs," the doctor stated. "Get the best medicine any doctor knows: sea air!"

Show Illustration #10

Some friends recommended that George go to the sea shore for rest, so George packed up his few belongings and made his way to a small fishing village called Teignmouth (show map if desired). Within a short time George's health began to improve. And so did his English.

NOTE TO THE TEACHER

The orphanage not only reminded George of God's provision, but of His love. Do you know that God loves you? Romans 5:8 says, "But God commendeth his love toward us, in that, while we were yet sinners, Christ died for us." That means that even though you and I are sinners and have disobeyed God, He has showed us His love by making a way for us to be saved from our sins through His Son, Jesus Christ. Isn't that amazing love?

George was very sick, wasn't he? That reminds me that the Bible teaches that you and I are sick as well, not in our body, but in our hearts. Jeremiah 17:9 says, "The heart is deceitful above all things, and desperately wicked." We are born with a heart that wants its own way rather than God's way. There is nothing we can do to cure our hearts either. Only God can help us, and He has through His Son Jesus Christ! We'll learn how in just a little bit.

George made several friends at the village's small Ebenezer Chapel including a young Scotsman named Henry Craik.

Henry had just become a minister in a nearby town. Despite both of their strong accents, they found a way to communicate.

"Your English is coming along well, George," said Henry as they strolled along the coast one day. "We'll make an English preacher of you yet!"

George laughed. "I don't know, Henry. There's so much I still don't know about the language or about the things of God. Sometimes I wonder how I'll ever teach others."

"Don't worry about the language. It'll come," Henry advised. "As for the things of God? Use the Holy Bible as your guide in all things, George. It will never fail you."

George listened and began to spend more time in simply reading God's Word–thinking about it, praying over it and using it to guide his actions. As George began to understand the Bible more, God began to give him opportunities to share from it. First George spoke at Bible studies and prayer meetings. But before long, he was being asked to preach regularly at the small churches that dotted the coast.

When he was finally well enough to return to London, he was filled with excitement about all the Lord had been doing in his life.

Show Illustration #9

But soon, the headaches and coughing returned. George also began to have concerns with the mission society. More and more God was burdening George's heart with the needs of the people there in England. But the mission society planned to send George somewhere else once his studies were completed.

"Lord, please show me what you want me to do!" he prayed.

Over the holidays he returned to Teignmouth for another break.

Show Illustration #10

As he and Henry Craik walked along the shore road, George explained his situation. "Henry, I've made up my mind. I'm going to write the society. I believe God wants me to preach the gospel here in England. I must preach wherever God leads me."

"What about the London Society, George? You're responsible to them."

"That's just it, Henry," George responded. "My first responsibility must be to God, not to man. Don't get me wrong, Henry. I'm thankful for the society. Without them, I wouldn't be here, but I must be free to do as God directs."

"Remember, George," Craik cautioned. "If you do this, it will mean they'll cut off your support. You're a stranger in this country. A stranger without any source of money."

"I know, Henry. I've thought about that too, but I also know that if I truly seek to serve the Lord and His righteousness, He will supply all my needs."

George smiled. "He's never failed me yet!"

With only a few shillings in his pocket to spare, George sent the letter.

Less than a month later, the response came. The society was thankful for God's leading in George's life, but they would no longer consider him a missionary student. They withdrew all support. Again, George's only hope was for God to provide.

That Sunday George was asked to fill in for the minister at Ebenezer Chapel. He had barely finished his sermon when one of the leaders came up to him.

"Mr. Mueller, we want you to become our minister here. Our current one is going to be leaving soon."

George was amazed. It seemed as if God had brought an answer to his prayer. Still he wondered how God could use him in a small fishing village with a congregation of only eighteen. Before giving his answer, he again went to God in prayer.

Show Illustration #11

A week later he once again stood before the congregation from the pulpit.

"Dear friends, I accept your offer, but on one condition. I won't guarantee how long I'll stay. My purpose is still to go and preach wherever God leads me. As long as He shows me His will is for me to be here, I'll remain."

It was a bold statement and several bonneted heads turned and bobbed up and down. As the people filed past him afterward, a few whispers could be heard.

"What do you make of that mouthful?"

"The nerve of that foreigner!"

NOTE TO THE TEACHER

Henry gave George good advice, didn't he? Do you know that Jesus will never fail you either? Jesus in God's only and perfect Son. He lived a sinless life here on earth unlike you and me. That means that He is completely righteous, or right, before God. The Bible says in Romans 10:11: "Whosoever believeth on Him shall not be ashamed." Whoever trusts in Jesus to be saved from sin will never ashamed or disappointed by Jesus because He never fails. Jesus has power to save.

Do you see how God was providing for George's needs? He provided George with friendship in Teignmouth and with godly advice through Henry Craik! He also provided George with opportunities to learn the English language and to share his faith. God says in His word, "But seek ye first the kingdom of God, and His righteousness; and all these things shall be added unto you." (See Matthew 6:33.) If you know Christ as your Saviour and are seeking to serve God, you can trust God to provide for your every need.

The next week some people didn't return, but several new people came in the weeks that followed. They wondered just who this preacher was with the German accent.

Show Illustration #12

A few days later it was George's turn to wonder about somebody. He sat sipping tea with Mary Groves, while on a preaching trip to the nearby town of Exeter. Her brother was a missionary whom George greatly admired.

"We expect great things from your preaching," she said sincerely and without a blush.

That night his sermon was not his best. Every thought seemed to come in German and became jumbled when he spoke it in English.

Yet afterward Mary was there to encourage him. "You preach what the Bible says, George Mueller, like you did tonight. He'll always talk through it."

George needed little excuse to make another trip to Exeter again. Despite her long nose and old age–past 30!–Mary had the most honest look and clearest mind of anyone he had ever met.

Up to now he had never really thought about getting married. He had always thought that a wife might even slow down his ministry efforts, but once again God was teaching George. Through careful prayer and meditation George realized that God had provided a wonderful helper in Mary. Her love and encouragement would not slow the work, but help to grow the work God had for George.

He and Mary were married in October of 1830. They soon settled into daily life back in Teignmouth, but something was bothering George. During a walk by the ocean one evening he revealed his thoughts to Mary.

It was the pew rent system. Like many places, the little church had a custom of collecting money for the use of each pew. Whoever could pay the best price got the best seats. To George the practice was anything but Christian. It made people like deaf Mr. Kennedy, who was poor, sit behind a spot where he could barely read the lips of the preacher. George saw only one solution: the church needed to get rid of pew rents.

"But George," Mary explained slowly, "the pew rents are how the church is supported. It's your salary."

"Exactly, Mary. If the pew rents are my salary, then it's up to me to decide whether or not to rent the pews."

Mary knew there was no changing George's mind, especially when he knew it was the right thing to do.

Show Illustration #13

A week later they made their way up the road to the chapel under a November moon. George carried a small wooden box and a hammer. Mary carried the nails. It took less than five minutes to nail the small wooden box at shoulder height on the back wall of the church. It took less than a minute to hang the sign over it.

It read:

> Henceforth, the minister will be supported only by contributions placed in the box by generous Christians.
>
> He will not at any time, nor for any reason, ask any man for financial sustenance.
>
> He will ask only God.

"How do you feel, George?" Mary whispered.

"Like I'm suddenly set free of everything and everybody to be the person God wants me to be. Something wonderful is going to happen to us, Mary. But what it is, I don't know yet!"

Several months later George didn't feel quite so free. He made his way back up the road to the chapel under the cover of darkness. He always waited for the deacons to bring him the money from the collection box, but tonight he just needed to be sure God would provide. It had been a tight week.

Show Illustration #14

He knocked on the bottom of the box. All he heard was the sound of his knuckles against the thin wood. He knocked again, harder. But he heard no coins jingle inside.

"Nothing!" George said with surprise and knocked again. "Empty! Nothing!" He turned out the lamp and the church became completely dark. He stood still, looking across the empty pews to the altar. "Lord, has it come to this?" he said out loud. "Nothing for George Mueller?"

Back home George looked at Mary already asleep in bed. What had his faith done for the one he loved. Would his determination to trust only God starve her? Was he being irresponsible? Then he knew what he needed to do.

NOTE TO THE TEACHER

Once again God had provided for George, hadn't He? He provided George with a godly wife just at the right time. Maybe you're worried about something in the future because you don't know how the need will be met. Remember, if you are a Christian and are seeking to do God's will, you can trust God to provide for your every need. He may not provide in the way you expect or when you expect it, but trust Him to provide in His way and in His time.

Why do you think George could trust God to provide for his needs without the pew rent system? He could trust God, because God had already supplied George's greatest need–to be saved from his sin. God has done that for you, too, by sending His perfect Son Jesus Christ to come to this earth and to die on the cross for your sin. He not only died, but three days later He rose again and lives forever! If you've never trusted in Jesus to save you from your sin, you can do it today.

He gave Mary a nudge. "Wake up, Mary."

She woke up reluctantly. "George, are you sick?"

"We need to pray, Mary."

"What is it, George. What's wrong?"

She slid to her knees next to George at the side of the bed.

George took her hand. Then quietly he spoke to God. "Father, all we are comes from You. All we have. This is the promise we hold to, and we won't give it up. If You are holding back from us because of some sin, cleanse our hearts. Speak to us. And then, O great God, supply our need."

The next morning at breakfast they heard a knock at the door. It was deacon Thornberry from the church.

Show Illustration #15

"Here pastor. I meant to bring this money from the box over sooner, but I was almost ashamed to bring it because it was so little–only one pound, eight shillings."

George could hardly contain the joy in his heart. "Thank you, deacon. Never be ashamed of it. It's God's money."

And that was the way it went. When George got down to his last few coins in April, somebody dropped some money in Mary's handbag on the train. One night when they had no bread or money to buy it, a woman they had never seen before knocked on the door and handed them a fresh-baked loaf. By the end of the year George had received three times the amount he would have gotten from pew rents!

That was why Mary was surprised one Saturday night when George said, "Mary, tomorrow I'm telling the folks at Ebenezer that my time with them is about up."

George's friend, Henry Craik, had recently moved to the city of Bristol and had asked George to join him as he started a new church work in the middle of the slums.

"You remember the agreement I made with the people, Mary? When I feel God is calling me elsewhere, I will go."

"But now, George? We're doing so nicely. The church is growing, and God is providing right here."

"And He can in Bristol too, Mary."

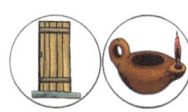

"I know George. It's just that it's not going to be just us anymore. By September the baby will be here."

Review Questions

1. When George was in school, he decided to ask only God for money. How did God answer his prayer? *(He sent Dr. Hodge, who paid George to be his tutor.)*

2. To what different country did George go so he could learn to be a missionary? *(England)*

3. What happened to George as he was studying in London? *(He got very sick.)*

4. While he was resting, George's friend Henry Craik told him to do something very important so he could learn more about God. What was it? *(Read his Bible and obey it)*

5. George realized God wanted him to preach in England, but what did the mission society say about that? *(He couldn't be their missionary anymore, and they wouldn't give him any more money.)*

6. When the people at Ebenezer Chapel asked George to be their pastor, what did he say? *(Yes, but only until God told him to go somewhere else)*

7. Instead of charging people money to rent the pews at his church, what did George decide to do? *(He decided to ask only God for money and to put up a box where people could give money if they wanted to.)*

8. Whom did George and Mary tell that night when there was no money in the box? *(Only God)*

9. What happened every time George and Mary were almost out of money or food? *(God sent someone to give them what they needed.)*

10. What was George thinking about doing at the end of the chapter? *(Going to Bristol to work with his friend)*

NOTE TO THE TEACHER

Do you think George will decide to go to Bristol or not? It was certainly a big decision. Maybe today you have an important decision to make. Perhaps you've realized that you are a sinner and deserve God's punishment for your sin, but you also understand that Jesus Christ, the perfect Son of God, died on the cross and took the punishment for your sin. You believe that He rose again from the dead and you would like to place your trust in Him today. I'd like to give you the opportunity to talk to someone about that right now. (Give instructions.)

If you do know Christ as Saviour already, I want to encourage you to seek God's will for your life. He has a special plan just as He did for George Mueller. You might be worried about how your needs will be met if you follow God's direction. Remember what the Bible says in Matthew 6:33: "But seek ye first the kingdom of God, and His righteousness; and all these things shall be added unto you." If you know Christ and are seeking to do God's will, you can trust Him to supply your every need in His time, in His way.

Chapter 3
PROTECTION AND DIRECTION

George had made his decision.

He and Mary would leave peaceful Teignmouth to help his friend Henry Craik reach the people of Bristol (show map if desired). Gideon Chapel was located in the middle of the slums. The garbage-filled streets of the city were far different from the peaceful English coast. But even George's imagination had not prepared him for what he would face that first summer in Bristol.

George and Henry had just left the house of a sick man when George spoke up.

"Henry, listen to me. That man in there," he said. "His skin was yellow."

"He did look rather poorly, didn't he, George?" Henry replied.

"You don't understand. I've seen that look before when I was in London. Henry, that man has cholera!"

Cholera, the dreaded disease, had already spread through London causing an epidemic.

 Before either man could say another word, they heard it. In the distance a single bell tolled–for a funeral. Cholera had come to Bristol.

Show Illustration #16

All that summer the bells tolled again and again as people died from the disease and sweltering heat. Inside Gideon Chapel the people prayed for deliverance. George and Henry saw more than ever the need to tell people about Jesus. Despite the epidemic they continued to visit the sick and dying.

At home, Mary was almost hysterical with fear as George prepared to go out once more.

"George, please don't go. You didn't come here to kill yourself. What can you do anyway?"

"We can pray, Mary."

"But you've already prayed. Every morning for two hours, you've prayed. Two hundred of you at the church. It hasn't stopped the epidemic."

"Nobody from the church has died . . ."

"What about the baby, George? It will be here in less than a month. Suppose you died. Please stay home, George!"

George gently took Mary's hand to calm her. Together they again knelt in prayer.

"Dear Lord," George began. "We ask for your protection over us . . . but if we should die even this night from cholera, our only hope and trust is in the blood of Jesus Christ who died for our sins."

 George soon hurried down the street as the funeral bells continued to moan across the city.

Finally, by October the epidemic was over. From the Gideon Chapel only one member had died. George and Henry led the church in a special service of thanksgiving for God's protection.

George and Mary had more to be thankful for, though. Their baby had been born. Lydia was healthy and Mary said she looked exactly like George. Life in Bristol was just starting to become normal when one day George received a letter meant to reshape their lives. It was an invitation for both George, Henry and their families to sail at once to Baghdad as missionaries. There was also money to cover the costs.

George had always dreamed of going to a far-off exotic place like Baghdad. He thought of the city: ivory and perfume traders, oriental music, ancient sites. It was a far cry from the Bristol slums. He was deep in thought one afternoon as he strolled down the street.

Show Illustration #17

"'ey Sir, can you give us a handout?"

The voice brought George back to reality.

From behind an immense iron fence a boy grinned at him.

" 'ow about a shilling?" The boy stretched out a hand, pressing a grimy face to the bars.

As George reached in his pocket for a shilling, he realized that he was next to an almshouse. The boy was an orphan.

NOTE TO THE TEACHER

Cholera was a dreadful disease that killed thousands and thousands of people. But do you know there is something even worse than cholera that we all have? It's called sin. Sin is our rebellion against God. It is the things we say, think or do that go against His ways, His laws. You and I and all people have sinned. The Bible says we deserve death because of it. Romans 6:23 says, "For the wages of sin is death." What we deserve is not just the death of our body, but the spiritual death which is separation from God forever in a real place called Hell. That's bad news, but there's good news I want to share with you, too. Keep listening.

 George didn't know if he would die from cholera or not, did he? However, he did know where he would go if he died. He'd be in Heaven with God because he'd put his trust in Jesus Christ. He knew that Jesus had died on the cross to take the punishment for George Mueller's sins, just as He had for you and me. George Mueller had also believed the truth that Jesus had risen from the dead and lives today. In John 14:6, Jesus said, "I am the way, the truth, and the life: no man cometh unto the Father, but by me." George trusted in Jesus alone to save him from sin, and so he knew he'd be with God the Father in Heaven if he died. What about you? Do you believe Jesus died for your sin and rose again? Are you trusting in Him alone to save you from the punishment for your sin? If not, I want you to listen carefully as we continue our story.

George thought back to Francke's orphanage in Halle. Unlike that one, the huge building before him appeared bleak and sad.

Suddenly wild laughter echoed from the building. It grew louder then choked off for a minute and then began again, higher, wilder.

The boy shrugged. "Just an ol' looney. Don't be scared. Where's my coin?"

What good would one shilling do? George dropped it into his hand. The boy would grow up there, caged with lunatics and criminals, while George Mueller slipped him a single shilling and sailed off to exotic marketplaces.

From that moment on George knew he would not go to Baghdad. But he would not be content to simply preach from the Gideon Chapel pulpit either. There was great need right in his neighborhood.

One night after supper, George told Mary, "I believe God wants me to start a day school, Mary. Not one like the other free schools though. This one will be run only by Christians and will give the children the right kind of Bible teaching too."

Mary held baby Lydia in her arms. "George, you don't have the money," she said finally.

George's enthusiasm was unwaivering. "God can provide it, Mary. I know it."

"But George, be honest. How much money do we have in this house?"

They both knew. There was only one shilling: just one shilling to start a school. To feed the children. To provide Bibles. But George had faith that God would provide.

By April, George knew something had to happen. There was little money to start the school. He spoke honestly and simply to God in prayer about the need.

"God, I know that you want me to start the school. But if I don't get money soon, I'll have to give up the plan. God, if I could have £20–it's a lot, I know–I'd buy some Bibles for the children. It would be a start."

Before the day was over, a woman came to their door. She handed George an envelope.

Show Illustration #18

"I'm sorry it isn't more, Mr. Mueller."

George counted it: £5, £10, £15,–£20!

"Madam, would you like us to spend this on something special?" George asked.

The woman hesitated. "Well, if it's all right to say . . . "

"Yes, go ahead."

"What I had in mind was Bibles."

After she was gone, Mary came running from the kitchen to the parlor.

"I heard everything, George. I'm sorry. I've been wrong. God wouldn't have sent the money if it wasn't His will for you to start the school."

Together they knelt and prayed in thankfulness to God for what He had done.

Soon the day school was established and filled with children. Poor boys and girls from throughout Bristol received a little bread to feed their stomachs and then heard Bible lessons to feed their souls.

But there was a problem. It seemed as if just when a boy began to understand his sin and his need of a Saviour, he got taken off to a poorhouse and was never seen again.

"We have to do something!" George said to Mary.

"But what, George? These children have no parents. The poorhouse feeds them and gives them a bed. What can we do? We're not running an orphanage."

". . . No, we're not . . . but maybe we should be."

Orphanages were a radical idea in England. There were only three in the whole country and none in Bristol. Still, the idea remained in George's mind for the next several months. During that time, Mary's missionary brother returned from East Indies. He had plans to go to Germany to recruit new missionaries. George agreed to accompany him as an interpreter (Show map if desired).

It had been six years since George was there. Their coach rattled through the town of Halle where George had accepted Christ. Dr. Tholuck from the university was still there. He and George quickly caught up on the past years. Before leaving, George asked Dr. Tholuck if he knew of a young man who was a friend of his family. He did and even knew where he was living.

"Tomorrow I'll take you to his room. He's staying at the Francke orphanage on the same floor where you used to live."

Was this a coincidence? Had he come all the way to Germany and Halle to have the Francke orphanage brought back to his mind? "O God, what are you trying to say to me?" was his heart's cry.

Back in Bristol, God continued to direct George's thoughts. One afternoon he had tea with a widow from the Gideon Chapel congregation. George's mind was filled with the responsibilities of the day, and the meeting seemed more like a distraction than of any real purpose. While the widow fixed the tea cart in the other room, George scanned the titles on the bookshelf nearby.

NOTE TO THE TEACHER

George knew that the boys and girls in Bristol needed help. They needed food and education, but they also needed something greater. They needed to know Jesus. Maybe you don't know who Jesus is. I want you to know that He is the Son of God and that He is without sin. He came to this earth and lived a sinless life. That's why He could take our sins upon Himself when He died on the cross. He had no sin of His own. He is God's one and only perfect Son.

Isn't it amazing to see how God was directing George's thoughts? That's the same God who lives today and wants to help you know what to do. If you are submitted to Him, you can trust Him to provide you direction for your life! Psalm 37:23 says, "The steps of a good man are ordered by the Lord." If you are obedient to God, you can trust Him to direct your steps.

Then his eyes caught it. There was the biography of Francke from Halle! He had already read it twice before, each time moved by the faith of the man who had dared to build an orphanage. The man had no money; he had simply asked God to send it to him, and God had.

At the end of the week he went to Henry Craik's study to explain his plan. Before entering, George prayed, "Lord, you know my heart. If this is not from you, please teach me through my brother Henry."

Show Illustration #19

Henry listened carefully as George explained his plan.

"Listen, Henry, we could get one of those cheap big houses right in the middle of Bristol. There would be plenty of room for 20 or 30 orphans. Then we could clothe them, feed them, educate them and show them the gospel."

". . . what about the money?" Henry asked.

"We'd do the same thing that God has taught us to do personally. We'd ask Him to provide."

Henry raised his eyebrows. "You mean, we don't ask anyone for the money?"

"Right . . . Henry, do you remember how during the cholera epidemic, our people really trusted God for help?"

"Yes," Henry replied. "We all knew that He alone could help us."

"But then, what happened after the epidemic ended? People went back to trusting in themselves, trusting in man's ways."

"What's your point, George?"

"The orphanage is the point, Henry! If I, a poor man, simply by prayer and faith, receive what I need to establish and run an orphanage, there would be something visible that the Lord might use to show Christians and non-Christians that He is still faithful and still answers prayer!"

Henry remained silent for a moment. Then with a smile forming on his lips, he spoke. "I think . . . that it's a wonderful idea, George."

Show Illustration #20

From the pulpit it was hard to tell how the Gideon Chapel congregation took George's announcement that he was going to start an orphanage. He didn't have to wait long to find out, though. As soon as he closed in prayer, there was a rush of people down the aisle to meet him.

Some were skeptical. "It's a newfangled idea!"

"It sounds like a hairbrained scheme."

Some were opposed. "The almshouses are good enough!"

"Bristol got along fine before you got here."

But some trusted that God was in it. "Here are ten shillings, Pastor Mueller. It's not much, but it's a start."

"I can cook and clean and I get along wonderful with children. Can you use me?"

George saw in these faithful few the fulfillment of God's promise. He had read in Psalm 81:10: "Open thy mouth wide and I will fill it." George had opened his mouth wide, wide enough to ask God point-blank for a list of specific needs. God had not refused him, but answered those needs one by one.

However George's joy was lessened by one thing. Mary still doubted.

Not long after, a letter arrived. It was from a couple offering their services to George. And, they even offered all the furniture they owned to help furnish the orphanage.

"I don't understand it. They don't even know you, George," Mary said.

"We know the same Christ. That's enough, Mary."

"Ten shillings, a cook and a couple, plus furniture for the house and you haven't asked anybody for anything?" Mary's voice quivered. "It must—there's only one thing to think. God wants it that way."

"Yes, Mary. Believe with me."

"I . . . I think I can."

Together they prayed again to God, thanking Him for what He had done and asking Him to continue to provide what was needed.

A bang came from the back door. George swiftly rose to his feet and answered the door. A man George had never seen set several bundles on the floor and simply said, "For your orphans."

Before George could answer, he was off into the night.

Together George and Mary tore open the packages and unwrapped the contents.

Show Illustration #21

Twenty-eight dinner plates! Three big servers! Three wash basins! Drinking mugs! Three salt holders! A grater! Four knives and five forks!

From out of the night a complete stranger had brought what they needed right to their door. How

NOTE TO THE TEACHER

Once again God was directing George's thoughts and actions. One way God provides direction is through wise counsel from others who know and love God. Proverbs 12:15 says, "The way of a fool is right in his own eyes: but he that hearkeneth unto counsel is wise." Think about the wise counselors God has provided for you (parents, pastors, teachers). Are you willing to listen to their counsel or do you want to do only what you think is best? If you are submitting to God, you can trust God to provide you with direction through wise counselors. Listen to them!

Have you ever thought about all the things that God has provided for you? What are some things you have enjoyed even today that are from God? *(Food, shelter, clothing, protection, health, etc.)* All these things remind us of God's love. He loves us, not because we deserve it. Very often we forget to thank or even acknowledge God's provision of these things, yet He still loves you and me. He loves us because He is love. In His love He has also provided for our greatest need–to be saved from our sin.

did he know that they had prayed that morning for kitchen things? Only God could have provided for them in this way.

In the months that followed, they continued to pray and God continued to provide.

They prayed for money. God sent it, even £100 by a merchant who had first acted irritated by George's idea!

They prayed for clothing for the children and someone donated material.

They prayed for helpers, and a housekeeper volunteered.

And they prayed for a house. God provided that too. It was a huge house on Wilson Street.

Show Illustration #22

George beamed as he gave Mary the news. "It's just aching to have 30 children move right in and slide down the banisters and shout from the attic to the back pantry!"

By the beginning of February it was ready for them to move in. It looked almost exactly like all the other houses on the street. But as George swung open the doors of 6 Wilson Street on the morning of February 3, he knew it was different. From that day on there wouldn't be a house like it on the street, not in Bristol, nor anywhere in England.

He sat down at a small table in the front room. The orphanage was now open for anyone to walk in and make application for a homeless child. George soon expected the room to be crowded with applicants.

He sat arranging papers and daydreaming for a half hour. Finally he walked over to the front door and looked out the front door. Nothing.

Show Illustration #23

He went back and sat for an hour and concentrated on bookkeeping and then began to feel uneasy.

Again at the window, he looked up and down the street. An old woman approached but then continued past the house. When she stopped a well dressed gentleman, George realized she was a beggar. The gentleman continued by the house as well.

By late afternoon, George had to admit the truth. No one was coming.

In his mind he could hear his critics. "Didn't we tell you? Doesn't this prove it? Bristol isn't ready for a newfangled orphanage yet."

George stood again at the open door in the front hall. "I don't know. I just don't know," he said aloud. No one answered him.

Review Questions

1. What terrible thing happened in the town of Bristol not long after George and Mary moved there? *(The disease of cholera began to spread.)*
2. How did God answer the prayers of George and his friends at the Gideon Chapel? *(Only one person from their church died of cholera.)*
3. What happened that made George decide not to go to faraway Baghdad as a missionary? *(He met an orphan boy who lived in an almshouse.)*
4. What was the first thing George decided to start so he could help the orphans in his town? *(A school, where they could get food and learn about Jesus)*
5. Why couldn't some children come to the school? *(They had to go live at the almshouse because they didn't have anyone to take care of them.)*
6. Later George had a new idea to help the orphans. What was it? *(To start an orphanage in Bristol)*
7. When George was talking to his friend Henry, he told him they would ask only one person for money for the orphanage. Who was that? *(God)*
8. Not everybody liked George's idea. Who was the one important person who had a hard time believing that God would help them start the orphanage? *(George's wife, Mary)*
9. Name some of the things George and Mary needed for the orphanage that God gave them. *(Money, people to help, furniture, kitchen things, material for clothes, a house)*
10. What happened on the day George opened the doors for children to come to the orphanage? *(No one came.)*

NOTE TO THE TEACHER

What do you think it was that George was unsure of? (Allow responses.) Maybe he was wondering if God had really wanted him to start an orphanage or not. Could George trust God for direction? Yes, remember what the Bible says in Psalm 37:23? "The steps of a good man are ordered by the Lord." What are some of the ways God provides direction to Christians? (Allow responses.) He uses His Word, His Holy Spirit and wise counselors. If you know Jesus as Saviour, you can trust God to provide you with direction as well.

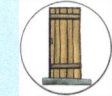

But maybe you're here today and realize that you don't know Jesus as Saviour. I want to tell you that God wants your life to change direction. He has provided a way for you to turn from your sin and to Him. It's by trusting in His perfect Son Jesus Christ who died for you on the cross. He took the punishment for your sin and rose again from the dead. If you trust in Him to save you from your sins, He will! Not only that, but He will guide and direct your path in ways that bring glory to God who loves you. Will you trust Him today?

Chapter 4
SACRIFICE AND BLESSING

"Nobody?" Mary looked up at George as if she were going to cry. He had just returned from the first day at the orphanage. Mary had been cutting out dresses on the parlor floor.

"Nobody came to 6 Wilson Street, Mary. Not a child." George slumped into a chair. "Not a grandmother. Not a city official. Nobody."

"Nobody applied?" Mary repeated. "Where were they?"

"I don't know. I don't understand it. Mary, I've truly examined my heart and I believe this orphanage is for God's glory and for the sake of the children."

"Yes, George."

"And God has always provided," George continued. "I prayed for money and he sent gifts larger than I dreamed. I prayed for kitchen things and a stranger showed up with his arms full. We prayed for cooks and teachers . . ."

". . . And they came, George," said Mary finishing his sentence. "You prayed for clothes and got them. You prayed for . . ." she stopped suddenly, her eyes widening. "Oh, George! George, don't you see? That's it. Everything you prayed for the Lord provided!"

Show Illustration #24

"Yes, everything. Except children."

"That's it, George. You didn't ask for children! We never prayed together for them."

George suddenly felt weak. She was right! He had prayed for everything else, but had always assumed there'd be children.

Next they did the only logical thing. Together in the parlor, they bowed their heads and asked God for the orphans.

The next morning, George woke full of confidence. He ate a quick breakfast and told Mary not to expect him for lunch. As he opened the front door of 6 Wilson Street he noticed two people on the pavement were watching him.

One was a woman whose bonnet perched like a giant bird on her frizzy, straw-colored hair. From behind her peered the eyes of a ten-year-old with a grimy face and grimy shirt to match.

She followed him into the house. tugging the boy behind her. George directed her to the little table in the parlor where he had sat alone the day before. After he pulled up a chair for her and sat down, he listened to her story. This was Jerry, her sister's boy. She had died, leaving him an orphan. There was no sign of the father.

Suddenly George jumped up in pain. Jerry, who had been busy exploring the house, had returned and dropped a large rock he had found on George's foot.

"Don't mind him," the woman said. "He's a good boy, down in his heart, if you can find it."

Show Illustration #25

George's morning soon turned busier as a half dozen women with about twice as many children came through the front door. Each peppered George with questions and explanations. Just as George was starting to restore order, he heard the crash.

Jerry had picked up the rock and hurled it through the parlor window.

"My window!" George exclaimed.

"Don't you worry, Mr. Mueller," one of the ladies shouted. "You asked for kids, didn't you? Well you got them, so don't complain none."

By May the orphanage officially opened. There were 42 children as well as cooks and housemothers to help care for the children. More requests came, though, and soon George had to rent a second house on Wilson Street to provide more room. By the following year he had rented a third house. During that time George kept his word and never publicly talked about money and never asked for a donation.

While God had provided for their daily needs, after two years George knew the situation was critical. One day, George knew they had no money left and needed £5 immediately. In his prayer diary George wrote, "God, I'm trusting You to supply it somehow."

A well-dressed woman arrived at the orphanage later that day with a few coins in her hand. She had been convicted about wearing fancy jewelry and decided to give the money from them to the orphanage.

"I know they're not worth much, Mr. Mueller–only £5."

"Not much? So much!" George answered, knowing that God had met their daily needs once again.

Still the orphanages continued to operate almost daily with nothing to spare.

NOTE TO THE TEACHER

Before they remembered to pray for children, George and Mary might have felt as if God had forgotten them. Maybe you've felt that way before. You've thought that God doesn't care for you because of who you are or because of something you've done. I want you to know today that God does care! He loves you not because of who you are or what you've done for Him. He loves you because of who He is. God loves you.

Have you ever heard anyone say something like that about you? The truth is that deep down in all our hearts is sin. Romans 3:12 says: "There is none that doeth good, no, not one." 'Not one' means that neither you nor I are without sin. We have all broken God's law and are deserving of punishment. But as we said before, God still loves us, and He has provided a way for us to be saved from our sins. I'll tell you how in a little while.

Show Illustration #26

One particularly wet and gloomy afternoon in September, George gathered the staff of the orphanage for a meeting. Until then he had never discussed the financial situation with the staff. He had felt that it would somehow be breaking his promise to God, but God was teaching him. He now realized that by not sharing the facts he had been robbing his staff of a blessing. He alone had been praying for the daily needs and had miraculously seen God respond. Now they would have the same opportunity. Still, he was unsure how they would respond to the news.

Calmly George explained how the orphanage was on the brink of closing despite everything they had done.

One woman stood and said, "It might help to cut expenses a little."

"But we have," George responded. "We've cut them to the bone."

"Not quite, Mr. Mueller. What about my salary?"

"What's that?"

"My salary, Mr. Mueller. The widow's pension I receive is adequate enough."

Another staff member handed George several pounds. "I'm heading upstairs to pray for our needs, but I couldn't ask God knowing I was holding this money back. Please take it."

Next, the cook spoke up, "Count on £6 from me. It's my extra savings in the bank, but I'm sending for it immediately. Now if you don't mind, I need to tend to the soup and get some praying in while it's simmering."

 George looked at the coins they had given. Their sacrifices meant so much, though it was so little. By the end of the week, even these gifts had been spent paying for groceries and bread from the baker.

Show Illustration #27

Soon George noticed a strange uneasiness in the orphanages. When he tried to ask two of the staff to help him move a bookcase, they hurried past him, out of the house, pretending they didn't hear. Their arms were full of bundles. He caught the housemother hustling out the back door. She was carrying something too.

That night George had supper at the orphanage. Suddenly one of the staff members stood up to make a speech. He stuttered out a few sentences and then pushed an envelope towards George.

Bewildered, George took the envelope. "Where did this come from? You don't have any money."

"It's an answer to your prayer. So the orphanage can stay open."

"Yes, but where did you get the money?"

"We had some things we didn't need."

"Things?" George asked.

"Things in our rooms. Silverware, pictures, a little furniture."

"You sold them?"

"That's right, Mr. Mueller. We didn't want you to have all the fun of having prayer answered."

These sacrifices again met the immediate needs of the orphanages and kept them open. However, in a few days the money was gone again. Except this time the houses were stripped down to the essentials, and none of the staff had any money left in savings. The only resource was God!

 And this was the last possible moment for God to provide.

Show Illustration #28

In the midst of the trial, George found himself seated at tea with a Mrs. Brightman, a widow from the church. She had come to George to ask for spiritual advice. George listened carefully, but as she spoke George noticed how worn her shawl and bonnet appeared. Had he become so focused on the needs of the orphanage that he was overlooking those in the church? The thought pricked his heart.

As she rose to leave, he spoke. "Mrs. Brightman, Mary and I would consider it an honor to share with you anything we have. Please consider what is ours, yours. Our bank accounts shall be one in the same."

Mrs. Brightman caught her breath and quickly pulled a handkerchief from her bag.

"You dear people. You dear people," she said wiping her tears. "You won't be sorry . . . you know I have £500."

Now it was George's turn to catch his breath. He had no idea she had any money!

NOTE TO THE TEACHER

 George and the staff members were praying that God would supply the needs of the orphanage, but they were also willing to give what they had to help. Do you know that if you know Jesus as Saviour, you ought to be a cheerful giver when there is a need? How much to give is a matter between you and God, but whatever is given ought to come from a heart of love for what God has done for you. Second Corinthians 9:7 says, "Every man according as he purposeth in his heart, so let him give; not grudgingly, or of necessity: for God loveth a cheerful giver." If you know Jesus as your Saviour, you ought to give cheerfully when there is a need.

 George and the orphanage had a great need, didn't they? Do you know that we have a great need too? It is to be saved from our sin. God has already provided for that need by sending His Son Jesus to this earth. Although Jesus, the Son of God, has always existed, like God the Father, He came to this earth at a particular time (about 2,000 years ago) and in a particular place (Bethlehem). He was born as a baby and lived a perfect, sinless life. Not only that, He did something wonderful so that you and I could be saved from our sin. I'll tell you what a little later in our story.

"That's not what I meant . . ." he said fumbling for words. "I mean . . . I . . ."

She quickly explained that she had inherited the money and had often thought about what to do with it.

"Your words have given me an idea, Mr. Mueller," she said as she departed. "Perhaps the money would be best put towards the work of the orphanage. Please pray that the Lord would show me what he wants me to do."

Show Illustration #29

Almost a month went by with no word from Mrs. Brightman. Not wanting to influence her, George made no attempt to contact her either. Instead he continued to pray faithfully for her and her decision.

Late in November, George came home to find Mrs. Brightman having tea with Mary.

Show Illustration #28

"Mr. Mueller, I want to share a common purse with you after all. The Lord has given me peace about giving up the money. I know He wants the orphanage to have my legacy–£500."

George cleared his throat. "I'm grateful," he began. "Very thankful. A little overwhelmed. But I can't accept it."

Mary set the teapot down with a clatter.

"Young man!" the widow chirped.

"Not yet. I want you to make sure it's what you ought to do. Please, take two weeks. Then, if He still has given you peace, the orphanage will accept your £500."

Show Illustration #29

And so George continued to pray. By the middle of December he received a letter from Mrs. Brightman. It said, "Since I last saw you, I haven't had the slightest doubt about what I ought to do. I've asked my heart if I'm really doing this for Him. My heart assures me I am. I want you to have the money. I'll forward it soon."

George and Mary rejoiced, but their wait was not quite over. The money transfer took almost three months. When it was finally settled, George had £500 in the Bristol bank for his orphans. God was already preparing in George's mind a most excellent way to spend it.

At the Wilson Street house, the housemother stood before George. He wasn't sure if it was good news or not.

"Thought you might like to know that the Grahams next door are going to move, sir. They thought you might want another roomy house for orphans. Of course I told them it's a pity you have no money."

George grinned as he thought of the £500 in the bank. Could this be God's plan?

Suddenly they heard a splintering and then an earthshattering crash!

"Now you've done it!" George could hear the scolding. "Broke it right in two!"

Broke what in two? The front door? Or a person? The boys were yelling now.

Show Illustration #30

George's questions were soon answered as he was presented with Colin–a ten-year-old orphan who had frequent visits to George's desk.

"What did you do this time, Colin?"

"Bannisters. Slid down."

"But what broke?"

"The banisters."

"The banisters? A thin fellow like you?"

Colin stuck out his lower lip. "Wasn't just me. About six of us. Made kind of a chain."

George continued his questions. As he spoke, George realized that there were a hundred other Colins amid the streets of Bristol. Boys and girls who not only needed food and shelter and a place to play, but who also needed to hear of God's love. Daily George was having to refuse applicants to the orphanage because there simply wasn't room. Now God had provided the resources and another home right on Wilson Street! God's direction was clear.

After Colin left the room, George quietly whispered a prayer, "Thank you, God, for sending me Colin today."

That summer 4 Wilson Street became the fourth house for parentless children.

NOTE TO THE TEACHER

Why do you think George wanted Mrs. Brightman to make sure of her decision? (Allow responses.) Remember the verse we looked at from 2 Corinthians 9:7? It says that we shouldn't give "grudgingly, or of necessity." George wanted Mrs. Brightman to make sure she wasn't giving because she felt forced or required to do it. He wanted it to come cheerfully from her heart. That's how we are to give too. If you know Jesus as Saviour, God wants you to give cheerfully when there is a need.

George wanted the boys and girls of Bristol to know God's love. I want you to know of His love too. God has shown His love to us in many ways. (Give examples.) But the greatest way He showed His love was through His Son Jesus Christ. In the Bible, John 3:16 says: "For God so loved the world, that he gave his only begotten Son, that whosoever believeth in him should not perish, but have everlasting life." God's Son, Jesus, lived a sinless life here on earth and then died on the cross. He died willingly, giving His life and His blood as a payment to God for the price of our sins. What is that price? We deserved death for our sins, but Jesus died for us. Not only that, but He rose again after three days. God accepted His payment, and God will accept you as His child if you trust in Jesus and what He has done for you.

Show Illustration #31

On the first day the doors opened, Colin and a new young boy ran in and up the stairs and then swished down the banister screaming all the way: "Hey, there, bully banisters! Bully banisters, Mr. Mueller!"

At the door, George shooed in the rest of the children.

Two little redheaded girls carrying dolls.
A boy with a face smeared with freckles.
A boy who blew a toy trumpet all the way.
A little girl with a cold.

The corners of George's mouth quirked upward out of sheer joy. Things had never looked so good for his experiment.

For two years all went along smoothly. Contributions came in regularly. Trouble over bills seemed a thing of the past, and the new staff members heard about it as if it were something that had happened before Queen Victoria's reign. There were now almost 150 orphans who depended on George for food and clothes.

Show Illustration #32

But trouble was brewing for George Mueller. One October day in 1844, in a musty house on Wilson Street, a man slammed his kitchen door and exclaimed to his daughter, "Them brats did it again, Bessie!"

"Another window, Pa?"

"Not just a window. The skylight!" He sank down into a chair. "That's the third thing them orphans 'ave busted in three months."

"You oughta get the law and order after them brats," his daughter said as she continued peeling her potatoes.

"They've ruined the street. Make so much racket a body can't sleep afternoons."

"What are you gonna do, Pa?"

"Write a letter."

"To the law and order?"

"No, to Mueller himself."

She flicked a few more potato peelings onto the table. "That won't do no good. Letters don't bother that stubborn German preacher."

"This one will. I've got a way to get 'em to close up every one of them houses! Now, go and bring me my pen, Bessie."

Review Questions

1. When no children came to the orphanage, George and Mary realized there was something they had forgotten to do. What was it? *(Pray for God to send children)*
2. Did God answer their prayers for children? *(Yes, soon they had to rent two more houses for them.)*
3. What did one lady sell so she could give the money to the orphanage? *(Her jewelry)*
4. At first George never told anyone except God about the money the orphanage needed. But then who else did he decide to tell? *(The orphanage staff)*
5. Name two things that the staff did to help the orphanage to have enough money. *(Gave up their salaries, gave all their savings, sold their things)*
6. When George offered to share his money with a widow from his church named Mrs. Brightman, what did she say? *(She had £500, and she would pray about giving it to the orphanage.)*
7. After a lot of waiting and praying, what did Mrs. Brightman finally decide to do? *(Give her money to the orphanage)*
8. After George talked to Colin, what did George decide to do with all that money? *(Use it to rent another house for more orphans)*
9. Why did a neighbor become angry with George? *(Because he said the orphans broke his windows and made too much noise)*
10. What was this neighbor planning to do about it? *(Write a letter to George and get him to close the orphan homes)*

NOTE TO THE TEACHER

It looks as if George is in for some trouble, doesn't it? Do you know that if you don't know Jesus as your Saviour, you face a much greater trouble than George did? In God's Word, Romans 6:23 says: "For the wages of sin is death; but the gift of God is eternal life through Jesus Christ our Lord." That means that what we earn or deserve for our sins is separation from God forever. But God has offered us life that lasts forever with Him in Heaven. To receive that gift we need to place our trust and hope for salvation completely in Jesus. He is the only one who can help us. If you'd like to talk to someone today about knowing Jesus as your Saviour, I'd like to give you that opportunity. (Give instructions.)

If you do know Jesus as Saviour, you have already received the most wonderful gift of all. You have the hope of eternal life, and real power over sin through Jesus Christ. Do you have joy in what you have received? If so, it should show in how you give. Second Corinthians 9:7 says, "God loveth a cheerful giver." God wants you to give cheerfully when you see a need.

Chapter 5
PATIENCE AND ENDURANCE

"But Father, a little noise never hurt anybody."

George strolled along the banks of the Avon River with his daughter, Lydia. She was now fourteen. Usually they played games skipping stones across the water, but George wasn't in the mood for games today. The letter from the Wilson Street neighbor was like a heavy rock in his pocket.

He wasn't as shocked by the neighbor's words about the noise and inconveniences as he was by the fact that he had never thought much about these things himself.

The last line of the letter kept coming to George's mind: *Sir, I leave you to judge the matter for yourself.*

George was thankful for his daughter. She was a good listener and having her to talk with always seemed to help him think more clearly.

He stooped down to pick up a smooth stone. "You and I forget, Lydia, that our own home is on Paul Street. That's a long way from Wilson Street and all the noise. The people there do have their rights. It's more than just the noise though. We have too many people in our homes. The drains on Wilson Street are always clogging and affecting the whole street."

"I don't know about drains, Father, but I do know that I never liked Wilson Street. It's ugly and all those houses are jammed together in a row. If I was an orphan I wouldn't want to live there."

Amused with his daughter, George asked casually, "Where would you want to live?"

Show Illustration #33

She pointed towards the north and treeless hills called the Downs. "I'd want to live in a wide open place with lots of breeze! A place with fields for playing. That's why I'm glad about that letter."

George looked at her in surprise. "Why's that?"

"Because then maybe you'll have to move the orphanages sooner to a place like that."

George knew for sure that Lydia was his daughter. She had a solemn face, straight mouth . . . and certainly big visions and ideas just like him.

"Lydia, if God gives us homes in the slums, then we should be thankful for them."

She turned to him and bluntly stated, "If God gave us so much already, why won't He give us a little more? A wide open place, I mean."

"Suppose He did give us land. What would you do with it?"

"Build an orphanage, of course!"

Lydia continued to chatter away, but George barely heard her. His mind was on what she had already said. To build a home of their own, instead of renting one. Perhaps she was teaching Him! In a moment he imagined an immense orphanage set up on the wide open hills of the Downs.

"Build an orphanage," he said out loud. "Why, of course. Bless you, Lydia. You're not impractical. You're just George Mueller's daughter!"

Show Illustration #34

For several days George carefully asked God if building an orphanage was His will. In his journal George wrote down any reasons he could think of for moving the orphanage or for keeping it on Wilson Street. Before long the answer from God was clear–they must move! But how? Next, George prayed his boldest prayer yet. "Lord, you know that we need to get out of Wilson Street . . ." He continued with the specifics. "We need about seven acres of land, someone to design and build a home for about 300 children, and £10,000."

For 36 days, George continued to bring his requests faithfully to the Lord.

And God answered! First, a donation for £1,000 came in. "That's the biggest donation ever given, George. How can you be so calm," said Mary.

"I'm calm because I prayed for it," said George. He knew that God would provide the rest too.

Next, God provided a Christian architect—a friend of Mary's sister. Not only would he design the home, but he also offered to come out and supervise everything, and wouldn't charge a cent for his services.

Then, in February of 1846, George heard about land for sale on Ashley Down, about seven acres. George knew this was the land God had for the orphanage. He hurried off to meet with the owner of the land, but somehow their paths never seemed to

---

NOTE TO THE TEACHER

George was certainly thankful for his daughter Lydia. Do you know that I'm thankful for a special Son? I'm talking about Jesus, the one and only perfect Son of God. He came to this earth and was completely obedient to God the Father. One day while Jesus was with three of His disciples up on a mountain, God spoke from heaven and said, "This is my beloved Son, in whom I am well pleased; hear ye Him" (Matthew 17:5). We are to listen to Jesus because He is the one and only perfect Son of God.

George knew He could trust in God because of God's faithfulness. Did you notice that George was also faithful to pray to God about the orphanage? How many days did He pray before God answered? (36) Many times we pray only once about something and then get impatient or angry when God doesn't answer right away or in the way we expected. Real faith in God means faithfully asking and waiting for God to respond in His time, in His way. If you know Jesus as Saviour, God wants you to pray patiently for His will to be done.

cross. George went to his home and found he wasn't there. He tried his office and found the gentleman had just left minutes before.

 George was puzzled and a little disappointed. He was about to hurry back to the man's house when the words of the Bible from James 1:4 came back to him: "Let patience have her perfect work." He decided to wait until the next day to find the man.

Show Illustration #35

When he finally found him, the gentleman looked tired and a bit upset. "Why didn't you come back last night, Mr. Mueller? I waited all evening for you. Truth is that I didn't sleep a wink last night. A voice in my head kept saying *Sell Ashley Down to Mueller. Sell it to him and don't even make a profit.*"

Before he knew it, the gentleman had offered George the land at an amazingly low price. George agreed. By the end of the year there was over £6,000 in the building fund. Some donations were as big as £2,000, but most were small, only a few pounds or shillings. Some were not even money at all. People sent George all kinds of things for him to sell, like rings, watches and knitted socks. One person even sent five stuffed birds! Some donations came from faraway places: like Switzerland, Australia and India. Some were from towns closer to home: like Barnstaple, Liverpool and Cornwall. Some donations came from the rich, some from the poor. Even the orphans helped by selling crafts they had made.

By the following summer George had all the money needed to start work on the building.

Two years later an orphanage stood on Ashley Down ready for the children to move in.

Show Illustration #36

On July 18, 1849, George and Mary stood on top of Ashley Down at the door of the new orphanage. A parade of 300 children walked up from the city to the wide open Down, where a southeast breeze carried the scent of the sea.

There were 120 orphans from Wilson Street and 180 new ones, brought straight out of the poorest parts of the city. The little girls passed by in their white capes and poke bonnets followed by the little boys in trim jackets, with visored caps on their heads.

"I'll never forget the last three and a half years, Mary," George said. "God provides!"

Finally the last orphan toddled up the front stairs and inside.

"Well, Mary, there it is. Our orphanage and our orphans–all 300 of them. It's all done now."

"Yes," Mary echoed. "It's all done now."

Before they could say another word, one of the housemothers burst out the front door.

"There you are, Mr. Mueller. I've been looking all over for you. No one can figure out the new gas burners–and the water upstairs. No one but you knows how to operate it. You'll need to come inside right away."

George began to laugh. "I don't think it will ever be done, Mary. God has more work for us to do."

Show Illustration #37

George was right. A year and a half later, he found himself sitting in his office at the new Ashley Down orphanage.

One of the workers appeared at the door. "Excuse me, sir, here's another one."

He handed George an application that had just been received in the mail. That made 78 orphans now waiting to come to the orphanage. And George knew there would be more now that the new building was finished. There were still over 6,000 orphans in the poorhouses of England! George couldn't help but think of all these who still needed food, care and shelter, but, most importantly, the good news of the gospel.

"We need more room, Lord," he prayed silently. "Room for at least 700 more children."

A thousand children all together! People would think George was crazy. Maybe he was, he thought, but the important thing was what God wanted Him to do.

So George once again prayed daily asking God to show Him what to do. Like before, he wrote down every reason for and against the expansion. So that no one but God would influence his decision, George told no one of his thoughts, not even his family. George had already figured that it would cost £35,000 to build the new orphanage and another £1,500 each year to maintain it. He knew if God wanted him to build, the money would come from the same place it always had, from God's faithful hand.

 At the end of five months, George was sure of God's will. Before telling anyone else, he first told Mary and Lydia.

NOTE TO THE TEACHER

 How do you think you would have responded if you were George? (Allow responses.) Do you ever get frustrated or angry because things don't seem to go the way you want? If we're honest with ourselves, we know that we've all thought or acted that way before. That's called sin and it's in all of us. In the Bible, Romans 3:11 says: "There is none that seeketh after God." In our own strength, not one of us follows God and His ways. Instead, we are controlled by our sin. We need real help from someone greater than ourselves. We need God's help, and you know what? He's provided it. I'll tell you how in a little while.

 Once again God gave George wisdom to know what to do, but it didn't happen right away, did it? George had to wait patiently. Although we like to have answers immediately, God has reasons for making us wait. Remember the verse that came to George's mind earlier? James 1:4 says, "But let patience have her perfect work, that ye may be perfect and entire, wanting nothing." God uses patience to build our faith in Him and to give us wisdom. If you are a Christian and seeking God's will, God wants you to pray patiently for His will to be done.

After listening to his plan, Mary simply nodded her head and said, "A thousand orphans! It seems impossible, George, but how can I doubt when we've seen God provide for us already in so many ways?"

Lydia spoke up too. "Father, I remember when the first orphanage was just a dream on an empty hill, but now it's real! God used that in my own heart to teach me that I could trust Him for salvation. Think about how many others might be encouraged to trust Christ through this work."

George smiled again. She really was George Mueller's daughter!

Next George prayed for provision. For the next few years he took Hebrews 6:15 as a Bible verse from God: "And so, after he had patiently endured, he obtained the promise." At times God provided abundantly like when someone donated £999 or when a single donation came in for £8,200! At other times the donations were scarce and small but never insignificant. Once he received six pairs of new shoes from a former orphan who now worked as a shoemaker. Another former orphan sent ten shillings and a note:

"Dear Sir,

Please accept this little gift from one who thinks of you and yours with thankfulness. I know it's a small amount and I'm sorry I don't have more to help with such a wonderful work . . . It was in the Wilson Street Orphan House that Jesus, the Light of Life, entered my dark soul. It was there that I first learned to call God my Father. For that reason I love the Orphan House, not only because it provided for my earthly needs, but because it is my spiritual birthplace. May the Lord reward you, dear Sir, for all you have done for me. I know He will."

After four and a half years George had his funds for the new orphanage building.

Show Illustration #38

However, he still needed the land. One muddy afternoon he set out with a real estate agent to survey a piece of land.

"That's it over there," said George as he pointed to a spot below the current orphanage.

"That's what?" asked the agent, shifting his clumsy record book from one hand to the other and easing one foot out of the ooze.

"The lot over there," George continued with excitement. "Check the boundaries. It should be large enough, don't you think?"

"For what, Mr. Mueller?" said the man staring at the barren hill.

"Why, for the new building!" George continued to describe it with its brick walls and six or eight gables, not noticing that the whole time the nervous agent was trying to get a word in.

Finally, when George stopped for a breath, the agent blurted out, "But Mr. Mueller! You can't build here!"

"That's what everyone thinks, but God has provided the money. It's all set."

"I'm afraid your money won't do any good. You see, the owner of the land is dead."

"Dead! But then what's the trouble?" George asked.

"Unfortunately for you, sir, the owner left a will that says that this land can't be sold or leased for a hundred years."

Suddenly George felt dizzy, and the new building in his dreams seemed about to crumble. But then he remembered the verse ". . . after he had patiently endured, he obtained the promise." Wouldn't God provide? If not through this land, then by some other means. There would be another orphanage building like the one set up on the hill . . . like the one up on the hill. . . .

George looked at the building. There it sat with nothing on either side of it but flat, treeless upland.

Suddenly, he was off, furiously through the mud, splattering his shoes and trousers.

"Come with me," he called to the surprised agent.

George carefully counted 200 steps on one side of the orphanage. "There must be 200 feet on the other side as well, right?"

"I suppose, Mr. Mueller, but for what?"

"For the building! If we can't build the new orphan house down there, then we'll build it up here–half on one side of the building and half on the other."

For every fresh difficulty, God gave George a solution.

By March 1862 the second and third orphan houses were completed. Now there were three buildings on Ashley Down. They were clean, square, and practically built with few ornaments. But they were not bleak and sad like the almshouses. To George they looked as solid as the gospel. To him, they were beautiful examples of how God had provided.

As the years passed, George could see that God was also providing for the future of the work. A serious-minded young man named Jim Wright began working at the orphanage and soon became George's assistant. George found himself praying earnestly for this young man to one day lead the work when he was gone. Lydia, now a grown woman, also had become a big help to George. Before long, George noticed that Jim and Lydia not only worked well together, but that their admiration for one another had blossomed into love. They were soon to be married.

NOTE TO THE TEACHER

In the note to George the former orphan called Jesus the "Light of Life". It says the same thing at the beginning of the book of John. "In him was life; and the life was the light of men." (See John 1:4.) Do you know that without Jesus, we would all be lost in the darkness of our hearts (sin) and facing eternal judgment in Hell? But Jesus, God's Son, came to this world and did something wonderful for us. He lived a perfect, sinless life in obedience to His Father and then went to the cross where He died for the sins of the world. That includes you and me. Not only did Jesus give His life as a sacrifice for our sins, but God the Father accepted that sacrifice. That means that if we trust in Jesus and what He has done for us, God will accept us too! He will consider our sins paid for, not because of what we've done, but because of what Jesus has done. We can fully trust in Him today because Jesus not only died, but also rose again and lives forever!

God had once again provided just what George needed. Do you think God ever got tired of taking care of George? (Allow responses.) Of course not. God loved George and loved providing for his needs. Do you know He loves you in the same way? He loves you even when you sin. In fact, that's why He sent His Son into the world to make a way for your sins to be forgiven. God loves you.

Show Illustration #39

There was another reason to rejoice on a day in 1870 when George and Mary stood once again on Ashley Down. Over 20 years had passed since they watched the children make their way into that first orphanage building. Now, instead of one there were five! God had allowed them to build two more orphanage buildings and to house over 2,000 orphans.

The wind buffeted them atop the hill, but they weren't ready to go inside the Home yet. This was a day for marveling.

George knew that on that day his monument to a God who still guides and protects life on earth was finished. George had accomplished the first and primary goal of his life. In all the years he had never asked anyone for a shilling! God had done it all.

Some had called George independent, a rebel, even a fanatic. Others who heard his story in another time, another place, would call him unrealistic and have their doubts. But to many more, it would be a sign. As he stood on the Downs that day, he was certain of that.

"They will know, Mary!"

She turned and looked at him affectionately. "Know what, George?"

"That God is faithful still and hears prayer still."

"Why, of course George."

With that he took her arm and led her to the door of the newest orphanage. But as they entered he paused.

"Mary," he said, "I think I know what God wants me to do next." And with that they went inside.

EPILOGUE

Your students may naturally wonder what George Mueller did after the orphanages were established. That same year, in 1870, Mary passed away from rheumatic fever and in 1872 George's son-in-law, Jim Wright, took over the operational control of the orphanage. But George didn't rest! Instead, in what he described as the "evening of my life," he began traveling around the world preaching the gospel and encouraging believers. God provided George with another helpmeet during this time in Susannah Grace Sanger, whom he married in 1871. From 1875 to 1892 they travelled over 200,000 miles on 11 preaching/missionary tours that included Scotland, Wales, Germany, Austria, Spain, France, the United States, Canada, Australia, Russia, as well as South East Asia and the Middle East. On one trip he even preached in the small town in Germany where he was born. On another trip he went to India, the country he had planned to go to when his father refused to sign the missions application. After returning to Bristol in 1892, he continued to help with the Bible school and orphanage until his death in 1898.

He died of natural causes at the third orphanage home on Ashley Down. At his funeral the city of Bristol came to a standstill as tens of thousands of people lined the procession route. Jim Wright spoke at his funeral from Hebrews 13:7-8: "Remember them which have the rule over you, who have spoken unto you the word of God: whose faith follow, considering the end of their conversation. Jesus Christ the same yesterday, and to day, and for ever."

Review Questions

1. What was Lydia Mueller's big idea for the orphanage? *(To build their own new orphanage on the Downs)*
2. Name one of the things George asked God to give them so they could have the new orphanage. *(Seven acres of land, a builder and £10,000)*
3. Name one of the ways God answered each of those prayers. *(People gave money; a Christian builder offered to work for no pay; and a man sold them land on the Downs for a very low price.)*
4. How many children came to live in the new orphanage? *(Three hundred)*
5. Was there enough room for every orphan who wanted to live there? *(No. Soon they needed more room for more children.)*
6. George decided God wanted him to build a new building. How many children did George want to have room for? *(Seven hundred: that would make 1,000 all together)*
7. Since George couldn't buy the land below the old orphanage, where did he decide to build the new one? *(He decided to build a new building on either side of the old orphanage on the hill.)*
8. After 20 years, how many buildings were there? *(Five)*
9. In all those years, had George ever asked anyone but God for money? *(No)*
10. What did George want people to know about God when they saw his orphanages? *(That God is still faithful and answers prayer)*

NOTE TO THE TEACHER

Do you think God is still faithful and that He still answers prayer? Yes, and if you've never trusted Jesus as Saviour, He's waiting to answer your prayer of repentance and faith right now. He promises forgiveness to all those who turn from their sin and trust in His Son, Jesus. Colossians 1:14 says, "In [Jesus] we have redemption through his blood, even the forgiveness of sins." Jesus gave His blood on the cross for your sins. He has risen from the dead and lives forever. If you believe that and trust in Him today, you will be saved from your sins and have new life and light in Jesus Christ.

If you have already trusted Jesus as Saviour, are you continuing to follow God's ways? God has a perfect plan for your life and you can trust Him to direct you. That doesn't mean that God always answers our prayers right away. Like George Mueller, we need to carefully consider God's plan for our lives by faithfully going to Him in prayer. The Bible promises that "they that wait upon the Lord shall renew their strength; they shall mount up with wings as eagles; they shall run, and not be weary; and they shall walk, and not faint." (Isaiah 40:31) God will not disappoint us if we trust in Him. If you know Jesus as Saviour, God wants you to pray patiently for His will to be done.